Genuine Faith

Also by Ed Cox

Grey Eminence: Fox Conner and the Art of Mentorship

Camping on Oahu

Travel With Kids: How to Travel With Kids Without Losing Your Mind

Genuine Faith

Thoughts on James

Edward Cox

Nomadic Dragon Media

GENUINE FAITH
Published by Nomadic Dragon Media, LLC
P.O. Box 11898
Burke, VA 22009 U.S.A.

All rights reserved.
Except for brief excerpts for review purposes, no part of this book may be reproduced or used in any form without written permission from the publisher.

Scripture quotations are from the ESV® Bible (The Holy Bible, English Standard Version®), © 2001 by Crossway, a publishing ministry of Good News Publishers. Used by permission. All rights reserved. The ESV text may not be quoted in any publication made available to the public by a Creative Commons license. The ESV may not be translated in whole or in part into any other language.

Library of Congress Control Number: 2024939112
ISBN 978-0-9971326-5-6
eISBN 978-0-9971326-6-3

© 2024 Edward L. Cox

Dedicated with appreciation
to my parents,
who taught me to love Christ,
and
to Paul and Stacy,
who enriched my understanding of James

Table of Contents

Introduction	11
1. What Really Matters (1:1-27)	15
2. Favoritism (2:1-13)	25
3. Faith and Works (2:14-26)	33
4. Taming the Tongue (3:1-12)	41
5. Wisdom (3:13-18)	49
6. Divided Hearts (4:1-10)	57
7. The Folly of Boasting (4:11-5:6)	65
8. Patience (5:7-12)	73
9. Prayer (5:13-18)	81
10. Saving the Wanderers (5:19-20)	89
Conclusion	93

Introduction

Faith. Prayer. Favoritism. Wealth. Speech. Oaths. James packs a lot of content into five short chapters. This book is full of practical wisdom on how to develop genuine faith. James was likely the first New Testament book written, and it hits with a bang.

James is my favorite book of the Bible, so it was a natural choice for me to write about. At one point, I had the entire book of James memorized. I carried it around in my head like a practical roadmap to a life of faith. Although I no longer can recite James from memory, pieces of it stick with me still. The verses I memorized surface at the most opportune times. I might recall James's warnings on the tongue when a caustic rejoinder is about to fly from my lips. I often think of his comments on favoritism when I analyze my feelings about other believers. I contemplate his advice about trusting in your own wealth as I plan my retirement.

The book of James provides guidelines on making faith visible through works. My intent in this book is a mid-point between a full, scholarly treatise of James and a superficial devotional. I hope this book helps you to dig deeper into the wisdom of James.

Authorship

Common tradition holds that James was written by Jesus's half-brother, James. Although James did not believe in Jesus while He was on Earth, James quickly became a believer after the Resurrection. At the time of writing this letter, he was the leader of the church in Jerusalem. Some consider James to be the first New Testament book written. Most scholars estimate the book was written between 45 and 50 AD.

The fact that James was written by Jesus's brother is one of the reasons I became interested in the book. I had two brothers and a sister growing up. I'm not comparing them to Jesus, although they are really great! I found the idea that James grew up with Jesus and still did not recognize him as the Messiah very interesting. Imagine if you had a perfect sibling, a sibling who never did anything wrong. You would think that would get your attention, right? But James and his brothers did not believe Jesus was the Christ until after his death and resurrection. Jude, another one of Jesus's brothers, wrote the book of Jude.

Acceptance into the Canon

James was not widely quoted by the early church fathers, but it was accepted as canonical as early as the second century. Both Origen and Eusebius listed it in their catalogs of New Testament scriptures. Eusebius noted James was disputed, but he did not list it among the writings he rejected. Eusebius also listed Second Peter, Second and Third John, and Jude as disputed.

Martin Luther did not like the book of James. He famously called it an "epistle of straw." He thought it conflicted with Paul's writings on justification as a result of faith alone (more about that in Chapter 3). Martin Luther also disliked the book of James because it did not explicitly mention Christ other than twice in passing (1:1 and 2:1). Even though Martin Luther did not like the book of James, he did not advocate removing it from the New Testament.

Three Themes of James

James is rich in detail and covers a wide variety of topics. These topics can be broadly thought of in three themes. First, there is the theme of speech. James spends a considerable amount of time discussing how our speech reveals our hearts. Second, there is the theme of contrasting worldly from heavenly. James compares worldly wisdom to heavenly wisdom. He also compares a focus on the things of this world to a focus on the things of God. Third, James discusses the connection between faith and works. This is the biggest theme in the book.

How to Use This Book

This book is designed for use by individuals for personal study and by groups for an inductive Bible study. Each chapter of the book analyzes a passage from the book of James and includes questions at the end appropriate for discussion or reflection.

One note about Bible chapters and verses. Chapters and verses were added to the Bible in the Middle Ages. Although the text of the New Testament is inspired, chapter and verse divisions are not. I've divided this book into ten chapters based on ideas or major topics in the book of James, which do not always coincide with the chapters and verses.

I hope you enjoy studying James as much as I have over the years. I pray this book will help you to identify practical ways to grow in your faith.

Chapter One

What Really Matters

(James 1:1-27)

The Author (1:1a)

James was a common name in the first century. In fact, there are four men named James in the New Testament. James the son of Zebedee and James the son of Alphaeus were both members of the Twelve. Another of the Twelve, Judas (also called Thaddeus) had a father named James (Luke 6:16). Finally, there is James, the brother of Jesus. This James is listed along with three other brothers of Jesus in Matthew 13:55 and Mark 6:3. Jerome, a 4th century theologian, theorized that James the son of Alphaeus and James the brother of Jesus were the same person, but there is no evidence to support this claim.

The book of James is commonly dated to have been written between 45 and 50 AD. James the son of Zebedee was martyred by Herod Agrippa I before the year 45 AD. His martyrdom is recorded in Acts 12:2, making it unlikely that he was the author. Very little is known about James the son of Alphaeus or James the father of Thaddeus.

The book of James is traditionally attributed to James, the brother of Jesus. This James was a leader in the church in Jerusalem as noted in Acts 12:17, Acts 15:13, and Acts 21:18. It makes sense that a church leader in Jerusalem would write to fellow believers.

The Audience (1:1b)

The letter was written to "the twelve tribes in the Dispersion" (1:1b). This indicates the intended audience was Jewish believers living outside of Jerusalem. Their meeting places in James 2:2 are described as synagogues, which supports the idea of a Jewish audience. The frequent use in the letter of the phrase "my brothers" is further proof that they were believers.

It may be that these believers left Jerusalem because of the persecution the church faced after the death of Stephen in Acts 7. Or they may have already been living outside Jerusalem and came to faith through the missionary journeys of the apostles. Either way, James writes to them because he feels a responsibility towards them as a leader of the church.

More broadly, this letter is written to believers everywhere. Its timeless wisdom provides practical advice on how to walk in one's faith with boldness and endurance. You'll note throughout this book I will refer to us as the audience, since we are reading and studying James together.

Endurance Training (1:2-12)

I ran a marathon years ago. I trained for months leading up to the race. Each week, the number of miles I ran during the week increased as I learned to build endurance. My final preparation for the marathon was a twenty-mile race two weeks before. I had never run that far at once in my life. But all the preparation was worth it. On race day, I knew I was prepared for the distance I had to cover because I had trained for it. If I had set out on race day with no preparation, it would have been a disaster. Instead, I enjoyed a pleasant but challenging run on a beautiful morning.

James starts his letter with a paradoxical word of encouragement – we should feel joy when we face trials. Jesus gave similar advice during the Sermon on the Mount (Matt 5:11-12). Why should we rejoice in these circumstances? Because it gives us a chance to grow in our faith. Genuine faith will become more persistent in the face of trial. Like a muscle, our faith grows as it is stressed and exercised.

What kinds of trials might we face? Maybe the trial comes in the form of persecution, such as the kind Jesus spoke about. Maybe the trials are inner moral tests. Maybe the trials are impatience as we wait for God to reveal His plans for us. James encourages us to pray for wisdom in all these circumstances. These prayers give us an additional chance to exercise our faith, for we must trust that God will provide the wisdom we ask for (James 1:5-8).

Trusting God during trials also means turning away from trusting in our own abilities. James reminds us that it is foolish to place our trust in our wealth. All earthly riches are temporary (James 1:9-11). The endurance James wants for us lasts beyond our lifetimes and outlasts our privileges and advantages here on Earth.

James echoes Jesus's Sermon on the Mount by calling those who persevere under trial "blessed" (James 1:12). The "testing of your faith" in verse 3 is mirrored in verse 12 by the words "stood the test." In both cases, the language evokes the image of proofing precious metals by melting them and testing their purity. The result is judged to be genuine. Peter uses the same language in 1 Peter 1:7. Precious metals are proofed by melting them. Once the gold or silver is melted, impurities float to the surface and are skimmed off. This results in a purer piece of metal, but first it has to endure being melted!

Victorious athletes in ancient times were awarded a wreath of laurel or other leaves to wear on their heads as a symbol of their victory. The reward for perseverance is a crown of life. Note that James emphasizes this crown of life is a promise from God. We can take comfort in that, because God keeps His promises.

Avoiding Temptation (1:13-18)

Denying responsibility is a very human reaction. Blaming others for one's temptation is the most natural thing in the world for humans to do. This isn't a learned response, either. Even young children will instinctively blame others when they are caught misbehaving. Eve blamed the serpent for tempting her in the Garden of Eden (Gen. 3:13). Adam blamed both Eve for giving him the forbidden fruit, and blamed God for giving Eve to him in the first place (Gen. 3:12). The urge to blame others when we are tempted, it seems, is part of our sinful nature.

James dispels this notion of blaming others, especially God. The words he uses in verse 13 are a command. When you are tempted, do not say it is caused by God. God is never the source of our temptation. James goes on to give two illustrations of how temptation works.

The first illustration presents an image of hunting or fishing. We are lured to temptation. When we see the lure, we are drawn to it. We are pulled away from the path we should be following. And to make matters worse, we're the ones to blame! We are baited, but the bait is of our own making. James tells us that the lure is our own lust (James 1:14).

In the second illustration, James switches to a comparison with conception and birth. When we give in to temptation and follow the lure, the lust we feel gives birth to sin. This sin results in spiritual death. Importantly, this passage also reminds us that encountering temptation is not sinful. It is only when we "take the bait" and are drawn away by our lust that we fall into sin.

In verse 16, James says don't be deceived. A better way of translating this is, "stop being deceived!" God is the source of all good things, while our sinful nature is the source of our temptation. James tells us to stop blaming God or others and to take responsibility for our sin.

Practical Tips (1:19-27)

Having dispelled any notion of blaming God or others for our temptation, James turns to practical applications of our faith. This section contains a series of short statements, each of which he expands on later in the letter. He focuses first on restraint, both restraint of speech and restraint of anger (1:19-20). The idea that we should listen more than we speak is not unique to Scripture. The Greek Stoic philosopher Epictetus is credited with saying, "we have two ears and one mouth so that we can listen twice as much as we speak."

James then encourages believers to sanctify themselves so they can grow in their faith with humility (1:21). The passage on hearing versus doing ends with an analogy of a man who forgets what he looks like as soon as he walks away from a mirror. This passage (1:22-25) is a good preview for the detailed discussion of faith and works in chapter two.

James 1:26 introduces a discussion on taming the tongue, which James continues in chapter three. This is also, of course, connected to his warning on restraint of speech above.

Finally, James summarizes his definition of genuine religion (1:27). Note that he discusses both external acts, such as caring for others, and internal acts, such as avoiding sin. Genuine faith puts spiritual truths into practice. The result is a life that is changed. This change is visible to others. The changed person seeks to glorify God, to love others, and to pursue holiness.

QUESTIONS FOR REFLECTION AND DISCUSSION

1. What does James say our attitude should be towards the trials in our lives? How often do you face trials with joy?

2. What does it mean to be double-minded (James 1:8)? How can one avoid being double-minded?

3. How does James encourage us to think about riches versus poverty?

4. What is a trial you have faced in your life? What helped you through this trial?

5. In James 1:13-15, what do we learn about the origin of temptation?

6. Explain what you have found helpful when dealing with temptation.

7. What do you do when you pray but still have doubts?

8. In your everyday life, how seriously do you take verses 19-20?

9. What does the life of someone described in verses 22-24 look like? What does the life of someone described in verse 25 look like?

10. What does genuine religion like that in verse 27 look like today?

Chapter Two

Favoritism

(James 2:1-13)

The modern English idiom "don't judge a book by its cover" warns us not to make our assessments of people based on their outward appearance. This sentiment is not limited to English. The same wisdom is conveyed in European countries by phrases like, "it's not the robes that make the priest," and "don't choose a dog by its hair." The terminology differs based on culture, but the wisdom conveyed is ancient and transcends language.

  This ancient wisdom reinforces what God told the prophet Samuel when he was directed to anoint David as king. God said to Samuel, "the LORD sees not as man sees; man looks on the outward appearance, but the LORD looks on the heart." (1 Sam 16:7b). If we are putting our faith into practice, we must seek to see people the way God sees people. This does not come easy to us. Indeed, it requires the help of the Holy Spirit to overcome our innate tendency towards judging by appearance.

The Sin of Partiality (2:1-7)

In this example, the believers treat the two men who enter the synagogue differently based on their appearance. They favor the one who they assume is wealthy and mistreat the one they assume is poor. The two men who come into the meeting are both visitors. They may be seeking to know more about Jesus. How the members of the church treat both of them reveals how the church feels about the relative worth of the different classes of society.

Having shown in chapter one the need to live out the spiritual truths we profess, James now moves from the general to the specific. He focuses in on a particular practice, the practice of partiality. Just as he did in 1:16, James tells us to, "show no partiality" in 2:1.

What's interesting about this command is the audience. Remember, James is not writing to a particular church, as Paul did in Colossians. James isn't writing to correct specific practices he heard were occurring, as Paul did in First Corinthians. Instead, James is merely observing human nature and noting the tendency to show favoritism is part of our human nature. But it should not be part of our lives as faithful believers in the Lord Jesus Christ.

The Royal Law (2:8-9)

James contrasts the practice of favoritism with keeping the royal law. The "royal law" is the supreme law. This royal law is to love your neighbor as yourself (Lev 19:18). As Jesus noted, the whole Law of the Old Testament is derived from the two principles of loving God above all else and loving your neighbor as yourself (Matt 22:36-40).

James doesn't mince words here. Those who follow the royal law are doing right. Those who show favoritism are committing sin.

The Law – A Package Deal (2:10-11)

There are some who might not see favoritism as being especially harmful. You might think, well it's not as bad, say, as murder or adultery. There is no spectrum of sin – all sin damages our relationship with God and requires repentance and salvation. We tend to minimize some sins as a way of justifying them to ourselves. And what's even worse, often the sins we minimize are the ones we are guilty of committing!

Because of this mindset, James further explains how favoritism equals complete transgression of the law. His example, however, is hypothetical. No one keeps the whole law and stumbles in just one point. As James notes, all of us "stumble in many ways" (Jas 3:2). But for the sake of argument, let us suppose someone had lived a sinless life with the one exception of committing one sin. Would that person be guilty of breaking the whole law? We have not just one example of this, but two.

Adam and Eve brought sin into the world with a single act of disobedience (Gen 3). I'm sure they continued to sin throughout their lives, but it only took one sin to condemn them and, by extension, the whole human race. So, can one sin cause someone to break the whole law? Yes.

God's law has many aspects, but it is essentially one thing. It is the expression of the character and will of God Himself. God commanded the Israelites to be holy because He is holy (Lev 19:2). Violating any point of God's law violates His will and contradicts His holy nature. Seen in this way, the sin of favoritism is far from insignificant. James ends this example with the sin of murder. This draws an even clearer connection between a sin which some might not think is too egregious, such as favoritism, and a sin that all can agree is a violation of God's law, such as murder.

Mercy Over Judgement (2:12-13)

James concludes this section with an exhortation to speak and act in light of the fact that we are going to be judged. The present tense of both verses calls for continuing action. James is writing to believers, so this judgment is not the judgment of salvation. This is the judgment seat of Christ, where Christ will judge all believers according to their deeds (2 Cor 5:10). The standard for this judgement is the royal law. We are empowered and called to love others because Christ loved us first (1 John 4:19).

The discussion of mercy recalls the poor man of v. 2. He came to the church seeking fellowship or compassion. Instead, he received discrimination based on his outward appearance. Those who have received mercy will show mercy to others, as Jesus explained in the parable of the unforgiving servant (Matt 18:23-35). Those who do not show mercy and love to others demonstrate they are not like Christ.

QUESTIONS FOR REFLECTION AND DISCUSSION

1. Have you ever felt underdressed for an event? How were you treated?

2. Do you regard favoritism as sinful?

3. When have you been helped by favoritism? When have you been hurt by it?

4. How well have you followed "the royal law" in the last week?

Favoritism

5. What is a practical way you can "love your neighbor as yourself" this week?

6. Why do you think the Bible often says it is easier for the poor to have faith than the rich?

7. Do you live as if you've been forgiven? Explain.

8. James commands us to show love and mercy toward others. How does this command relate to God's love and mercy toward you?

Chapter Three

Faith and Works

(James 2:14-26)

She stands in the middle of the road, just under a traffic light. Cars speed by going in both directions. On the ground at her feet is a small backpack, held together with wide strips of gray tape. Her jeans are dirty and ripped. With her right hand, she holds a puffy jacket closed because the zipper is broken. In her left hand, she clutches a piece of cardboard with a crudely written plea in large red letters. She smiles timidly at you as you pull into the left-turn lane and wait for the light to turn green.

Faith Without Works (2:14-17)

James moves back from the specific example of favoritism to the general principle of saving faith. True faith is revealed in a transformed life. Some scholars have argued this section contradicts the doctrine of justification by faith alone that Paul writes about (Rom 3:28). Indeed, even Martin Luther himself took issue with the Book of James for this reason. It probably didn't help that the Council of Trent, which was convened by the Catholic Church in response to the Protestant Reformation, cited James 2:24 as a counter-argument to the doctrine of justification by faith alone.

In v. 14, James argues a faith without works is not genuine, saving faith. He poses the question in a way that anticipates a negative answer, saying, "can that faith save him?" He goes on to give a vivid example of faith without works (2:15-16). All of us can see the uselessness of giving platitudes without giving assistance. James doesn't sugarcoat his position on this issue. Faith without works is dead. Not sick. Not lackluster. Dead.

Faith Shown By Works (2:18-19)

James makes this distinction even clearer. Someone may have works without faith, but it is not possible to have true faith without works. Faith is an inner attitude, but it is revealed by eternal works. Instinctively, we know this to be true in other areas of our lives as well. If someone tells you that she is a sculptor, you expect to see sculptures as proof. If someone tells you that he is a writer, you expect to see written documents as proof. Being and doing are not the same, but they are connected.

So, if someone claims to be a follower of Christ, we can and should expect them to be like Christ. And Christ loved people and helped people. There is not a single instance in the gospels of someone asking Jesus for help and not receiving it. Not once does he say, "I'll pray for you," and then walk away without also taking care of the person's physical needs. The life of a follower of Christ should have the same characteristics. We should help people, not just pray that someone helps them.

Intellectual understanding of God is not enough. One can admit the truth of the Shema, found in Deuteronomy 6:4, that there is one God, and still not be saved. James sarcastically mocks this idea by pointing out even demons understand there is only one God. This thought terrifies them, though, because they have no hope of salvation. Belief in God has not brought them peace with God. Peace with God requires a changed heart, and a changed heart will necessarily manifest with changed actions.

Abraham (2:20-24)

James continues his argument with a blunt statement. "Do you want to be shown, you foolish person," he says, "that faith apart from works is useless?" In verse 17, James called such faith dead. Here, in verse 20, he calls it "useless," meaning it accomplishes nothing. James then gives two examples of faith which is demonstrated by works. Abraham was declared righteous because he obeyed God in offering his son Isaac to God (Gen 22:1-18). During this test, the LORD said it was Abraham's act which demonstrated his faith in God (Gen 22:12). The LORD went on to say this act of obedience would lead to all nations being blessed through Abraham's descendants. This refers, of course, to Jesus.

Abraham believed in God, and God declared him righteous because of his faith. This declaration refers to Genesis 15, when God promised Abraham countless descendants through a son who was yet to be born. The events of Genesis 15 happened three decades before the story in Genesis 22. Abraham had faith, and that faith was proven in Genesis 22. As a result, James tells us that Abraham was called God's friend. This is a reference to Second Chronicles 20:7 and Isaiah 41:8.

Without context, it is possible to see James 2:24 as conflicting with Paul's statements regarding justification by faith alone. But with all of the context surrounding this verse, it is hard to see much daylight between James and Paul. Indeed, even Paul admits works are a necessary result of faith. In Ephesians 2:8-9, Paul declares we are saved by grace through faith which is not a result of works. But he goes on to say in verse 10 that we are created to do good works.

Rahab (2:25-26)

One might read the example of Abraham and think, "sure, Abraham had faith shown through deeds. After all, Abraham is the father of the Israelite nation." It's easy to look at others and think they are better examples than we are. But God calls each of us to live for Him using the gifts He has given us, in the locations where He has placed us.

To drive this point home, James gives a second example. The story of Rahab is found in Joshua 2. Rahab was a Canaanite woman, living in Jericho. She was a prostitute. God appeared and spoke directly to Abraham on several occasions. Rahab had never had any interaction with God or with the Israelites prior to the spies coming to Jericho. Rahab could not be more different from Abraham in terms of circumstances. But in terms of faith, Rahab is as good an example as Abraham. Rahab declares her faith in God in Joshua 2:11. She risked her life to save the Israelite spies. As a result of her actions, the spies are able to successfully return to Joshua and relay what they learned in Jericho. When the walls of Jericho fell, Rahab and her family are saved and protected. She lived among the Israelites (Josh 6:25). She is listed as a hero of the faith (Heb 11:31). She is an ancestor of King David and Jesus (Matt 1:5-6).

James concludes this passage with an analogy to the human body. Just as the physical body requires the soul to have life, so faith requires works as proof.

QUESTIONS FOR REFLECTION AND DISCUSSION

1. What was your first reaction to the description of the panhandler at the start of the chapter?

2. What kind of faith is discussed in verse 14?

3. According to James, what is the relationship between faith and works?

4. There are lots of unbelievers who live moral lives. Explain how works can exist without faith but faith cannot exist without works.

5. How do you reconcile the views of Paul in Ephesians 2:8-10 with James 2?

6. Why should believers live differently than they did before they were saved?

7. Which example do you think best illustrates the connection of faith and works, Abraham or Rahab? Why?

8. What areas in your life show strong signs of faith? What areas need improvement?

Chapter Four

Taming the Tongue

(James 3:1-12)

How many words does a person speak in a lifetime? I've seen estimates as low as 70 million words and as high as 800 million words. Despite the wide disparity between those two estimates, it's easy to grasp that humans talk a lot. And Jesus warned that we will be judged for every word we speak (Matt 12:36). It's no surprise, then, that James devotes a significant portion of his letter to warnings about our speech. In this chapter, James expands on and explains the warnings he gives in James 1:19 and 1:26.

The Responsibility of Teachers (3:1-2)

American historian Henry Adams said, "A teacher affects eternity; he can never tell where his influence stops."

This can be true about teachers of many subjects, but it is especially true about teachers of Scripture.

Teaching is a noble calling, but James cautions against it for good reason. The benefits of influencing the minds of others come with a responsibility to do so with accuracy and humility.

Jesus warned against being a teacher for the wrong reasons. He noted the scribes and Pharisees loved to be called Rabbi and all of the respect and honor that came with that title (Matt 23:6-8). Paul warned about people who want to be teachers but lack the knowledge to teach accurately. This lack of knowledge did not stop them from teaching falsely (1 Tim 1:6-7). Both of these warnings reinforce the message of James. If one is called to be a teacher of Scripture, that is a good thing. But pursue this calling with caution. Teachers will be judged more strictly precisely because they have great influence. This influence often comes from what teachers say, which is why this statement introduces the section on the power of the tongue. James includes himself in this group, saying, "we who teach."

Since sins of speech are the hardest to avoid, a person who could control his tongue could control all other aspects of his life (3:2). This person would be sinless. Unfortunately, James goes on to show that is not the case for any of us.

The Power of the Tongue (3:3-5a)

I love to sail. I first learned to sail as a teenager. I spent a few weeks at my uncle's house and he taught me to sail on a small lake in upstate New York. I love the feel of the wind on my face and the power as it pushes the sail. I appreciate the example James gives of a ship's rudder. Even a small twenty-foot sailboat can weigh several tons, yet it can be steered with a small piece of wood which weighs a few pounds. Others might have an easier time visualizing the analogy of steering a horse with a bridle. Both examples were common metaphors in ancient ethical writings. Both examples drive home the same point. The tongue is a small part of the body, but its ability to influence is vast.

We know instinctively that speech is powerful. God spoke the universe into existence. That alone is proof that speech is powerful. God also revealed Himself to us through speech, first to the patriarchs and prophets, and then through them to all of us when that speech was written down as Scripture. Lastly, one of the names of Christ is the Word of God. All of these facts emphasize the power of speech. That power can be used for good, or it can be used for evil. The speech of one person can inspire a person or destroy a nation.

Think about how the words of others have inspired or hurt you. Have you ever said something you instantly wished you could take back?

The Wickedness of the Tongue (3:5b-8)

James switches from the positive analogies to a negative one. The National Interagency Fire Center documents an average of 70,000 wildfires in the U.S. each year. According to the National Park Service, most of these wildfires are caused by human negligence through unattended campfires, discarded cigarettes, and other acts of neglect. The image of a wildfire starting from a single spark and destroying hundreds or thousands of acres is a powerful image. This is intentional. James wants to drive home the point that our speech can have tremendous negative consequences.

James doesn't say the tongue is "like a fire." He says it "is a fire." It corrupts the whole body. It is a restless evil. Examples of a wicked tongue include gossiping, bragging, lying, complaining, manipulating, false teaching, and putting others down. Of course, the tongue is not acting on its own in this regard. James speaks of the tongue, but our speech is decided by our minds. As Jesus said, our speech reveals what is in our hearts (Luke 6:45).

This wisdom about the impact of speech is not exclusive to the Bible. Many traditions and sources of wisdom discuss the impact of speech and the importance of guarding your tongue. What is unique to the Bible, however, is the wisdom that this guarding is impossible without the help of the Holy Spirit. We cannot tame our speech by ourselves. If we could, we would be perfect (3:2). But we cannot.

The Paradox of Our Speech (3:9-12)

James draws three comparisons to nature (3:11-12). A salt water spring cannot produce fresh. A fig tree cannot bear olives, and a grapevine cannot produce figs. In a sermon on this passage, preacher Charles Spurgeon noted the reason for this. A fig tree cannot bear olives because it is contrary to its nature. Trees can be identified by their fruit. In the same way, Scripture tells us that believers can be identified by their fruit. Spurgeon preached, "if the fig tree should ever bring forth olive berries, we might have good reason to question whether it was a fig tree, for a tree is known by its fruits."

James connects this question of identity to our speech (3:9-10). It is inconsistent to praise God and curse people, since people are image bearers of God. Suppose someone claimed to be a fan of Shakespeare but criticized every play and sonnet he wrote. You would have a difficult time believing that person was a true fan. In the same way, if people criticize, gossip about, and tear down others, who are made in God's image, it's hard to believe them when they claim that they are truly followers of God.

James doesn't accuse readers of being non-believers. He repeatedly calls them "my brothers." But, he points out they aren't acting in accordance with their claim to faith in Christ. As Spurgeon wrote, "when one who professes to be a Christian lives as worldlings live, there is grave reason to fear that he is a worldling not withstanding his profession."

QUESTIONS FOR REFLECTION AND DISCUSSION

1. Why is being a teacher such a burden, especially for teachers of Scripture?

2. What do the examples of the bit and rudder in verses 3-4 teach about watching what we say?

3. Is harsh language ever appropriate? If so, when?

4. According to verse 8, no one can tame the tongue. If that is true, how can we control our speech?

5. Discuss your reflections on the paradox of speech in verses 9-12.

6. What does this passage prompt you to pray about? Be specific.

Chapter Five

Wisdom

(James 3:13-18)

Again, James moves from the specific instruction about our speech to a more general discussion about wisdom. He contrasts earthly wisdom with heavenly wisdom. Earthly wisdom is not actually wisdom, but the use of the word "wisdom" reflects the Hebrew concept at the time of wisdom as practical rather than spiritual.

Evidence of Wisdom (3:13)

James continues to talk to those who seek to become teachers. Those who would be teachers must develop expertise in what they seek to teach. One useful contrast is to look at those who lack understanding. In 1 Timothy 6:3-4, Paul writes that those who teach false doctrine lack understanding. But James goes further, arguing that words alone are not enough. Having the knowledge and expertise is not enough. A person must demonstrate the truth of those words and the effect of that expertise by actions. James is continuing the theme from chapter 2, emphasizing that works must be present as proof of thoughts or words. He goes even further and now includes motives. The actions should be motivated by humility, not by pride or a desire for praise.

Earthly Wisdom (3:14-16)

James 3:14 might seem out of place. It starts with the word "but," creating a contrast with the previous sentence. Most of us would not quickly admit to having bitter envy or selfish ambitions. We almost certainly wouldn't boast about it. The construction of this sentence in the Greek indicates a situation that is present, not hypothetical. James is writing to believers everywhere, not to believers in a certain location. This means James thinks this situation is present in the lives of believers everywhere. James' admonition is particularly directed at those who would use the Christian faith or the church for their own selfish interests.

This is part of the struggle of simultaneously being saved and being in the process of being sanctified. We who know Christ live in a dual state, sometimes referred to as, "already; not yet." We are saved and forgiven. At the same time, we struggle with our tendency towards sin. James admonishes us not to revel in these sinful qualities. He also cautions us not to fool ourselves into thinking we don't have these sinful qualities either.

The "wisdom" in verse 15 is, of course, not wisdom at all. It is a perversion of wisdom. It does not come from above, meaning heaven. As James stated in 1:17, all good things come from above; from the Father. By contrast, this wisdom is earthly. It does not have an eternal perspective. It is focused on the here and now. This type of wisdom is foolish in the eyes of God (1 Cor 3:19). James builds to a crescendo with the three adjectives he uses to describe this wisdom. It is unearthly. It is unspiritual. Finally, it is demonic. And where there is sin of one kind there will be other sins as well (3:16).

Heavenly Wisdom (3:17-18)

Just as the earthly wisdom results in envy and strife, the heavenly wisdom results in peace. James gives a detailed description of this wisdom. In the section above, James built to a crescendo describing earthly wisdom. Here, he leads with the most important trait. Heavenly wisdom is pure. This purity does not refer to sexual purity. In this instance, the word "pure" means without moral defect or blemish. It suggests the absence of sinful motives. It's the same word used to describe God himself in 1 John 3:3. All of the other traits in this verse flow from this characteristic.

Heavenly wisdom is peaceful. It is free from anxiety or worry. It is gentle, or forbearing. This word is also used to describe God as forgiving (Ps 85:5). Believers should exhibit the same quality and be quick to forgive because we have also been forgiven (Matt 18:23-35). Heavenly wisdom is reasonable and produces good fruits. Again, we see the emphasis by James that true faith is proven by the works it produces.

There is truth to the old expression, "you reap what you sow." If you sow discord and strife, you cannot reasonably expect to reap peace. James ends this section with a call to be peacemakers.

QUESTIONS FOR REFLECTION AND DISCUSSION

1. Think of someone you consider wise. Why do you consider this person wise?

2. What behaviors lead you to think someone lacks wisdom?

3. Have you ever known someone who claimed to be wise but acted foolishly?

4. What do you think of when you hear the word peace?

5. When you find yourself in conflict, are you tempted to escalate the conflict or to seek a peaceful resolution?

6. Why is it important for believers to seek heavenly wisdom?

7. Compare the traits of heavenly wisdom in 3:17-18 with the fruit of the Spirit in Galatians 5:22-23. Discuss the similarities and differences.

8. Is it possible to be wise without the traits in 3:17-18?

9. Which traits from 3:17 do you most need to develop in your life?

Chapter Six

Divided Hearts

(James 4:1-10)

I mentioned in the introduction that James appealed to me because I have siblings. Jesus had brothers and sisters. Mark 6:3 lists the names of four brothers and mentions sisters (plural). They are also mentioned in Matthew 13:55-56. That means Jesus was one of at least seven children. If you have siblings, imagine if you never fought with them. Not occasionally. Not rarely. Never. Unbelievable, isn't it?

Now extend that to not quarreling with any fellow believers. To say this is a difficult idea is an understatement. And yet, that is the goal we strive for – harmony and unity in the body of Christ. In the last section, James contrasted earthly wisdom and heavenly wisdom. In this section, James delves deep into the worldly mindset to identify behaviors and attitudes we should rid ourselves of as believers.

Your Real Problem (4:1-6)

James doesn't ask if there is quarreling and fighting among the believers. He takes it as a given that such conflict exists. And James points out the root cause of these conflicts. The root cause, simply stated, is selfishness. The word in 4:1 for desires or pleasures is the source of the English word "hedonism," the philosophy that the main goal of life is personal pleasure. When we fix our focus on our own pleasure as our main goal in life, we inevitably come into conflict with each other.

When that selfish desire is thwarted, we lash out in frustration. We covet, quarrel, and fight. It doesn't matter if we literally commit murder or not (4:2), because Jesus taught that hatred is equal to murder (Matt 5:21-22).

James says we do not have because we do not ask. If we do ask, we ask for the wrong things or ask for the wrong reasons. Volumes and volumes have been written on prayer, so I won't go into much detail here on this topic. But it is clear from James 4:3 that the wrong motives include a focus on our individual selfish pleasure.

Seeking this pleasure is at the expense of the needs of others, or at the expense of obeying God, or both. For this reason, James accuses the readers of spiritual unfaithfulness by calling them adulteresses (4:4). James uses this shocking language purposefully to convey a truth found throughout the Bible – friendship with the world is the opposite of friendship with God (Matt 6:24; 1 John 2:15).

So, the difficult news is that God sets a high standard for our devotion to Him and demands our complete love and obedience. This may seem like difficult news, but it is not vague. James makes it perfectly clear that we cannot claim to serve God and continue to live worldly lives. Our inner life and our outer life need to match. This continues the theme of faith manifesting itself through good works. The good news for us is that God gives grace and mercy greater than the demands He makes on us (4:6). The solution for overcoming our sinful, selfish desires is humility.

The Real Solution (4:7-10)

Ever practical, James offers practical ways to develop this humility. Since God opposes the proud but helps the humble, we should seek to be humble. James gives ten commands in this section on how to develop humility; submit, resist, draw near, wash, purify, grieve, mourn, weep, change, and humble ourselves. These commands are a lifelong practice. We will continue to stumble and fall short. When we do, we can reflect on this list, repent, and rededicate ourselves to God.

We are to submit to God and resist the devil. Submission to God involves subordinating our will to His will. James assures us that if we resist the devil, he will flee from us. We can be tempted to sin (1:14), but all temptation can be resisted (1 Cor 10:13).

James also promises us that if we draw near to God, He will draw near to us (4:8). The command to wash your hands refers to one's conduct, while the command to purify your heart refers to purifying thoughts and motives.

James gives four commands in verse 9, and all four deal with repentance. Before, believers were focused on selfish desires, envy, and personal pleasure. Reflecting on that behavior should cause believers to grieve about their sinful nature. They should mourn and weep about the adulterous relationship they had with the world in defiance of God. The worldly things that caused them to laugh should now change to sorrow and gloom.

If one follows these commands, one will be humble before God. As James noted above, God gives grace to the humble (4:6). If we are humble, God will lift us up. Though we do not deserve it, God reaches out to us in love and imbues us with His righteousness.

QUESTIONS FOR REFLECTION AND DISCUSSION

1. Why is quarreling so bad for a body of believers?

2. Think about your prayers from the last week. How do those prayers compare to James 4:2-3?

3. How much of your prayer time is spent asking for things for yourself versus asking for things for others?

4. Do you pray for God to approve the plans you've already decided on?

5. How can we ensure we are praying with the right motives?

6. What are some practical ways to draw near to God this week?

7. Why should we want God to lift us up?

Chapter Seven
The Folly of Boasting
(James 4:11-5:6)

Have you ever been certain about something that turned out to be wrong? Have you ever had your plans for the future overturned by circumstances outside your control? In this section, James writes about the folly of thinking we know best, either about another believer or about the future. Both the hearts of others and the future are in the hands of God, not in our hands.

Don't Speak Against a Brother (4:11-12)

James commands us not to criticize each other. This command is usually translated as either "slander" or "speak evil against." The same word is used in First Peter 2:12 and 3:16, but in those cases it is the non-believers who are slandering believers. In this passage, James addresses believers who are engaging in this activity. Criticizing or slandering is part of several lists of sins in the New Testament (Rom 1:30; 2 Cor 12:20; 1 Pet 2:1). Why is this such a problem? James gives three reasons not to speak against another person.

First, Jesus summarized the law as love for God and love for our neighbors (Matt 22:37-40). When we fail to love our neighbors, we are breaking God's law. Criticizing one another is not showing love.

Second, James tells us that judging another believer reveals our thoughts about the Law itself. When we put ourselves in a position to judge others, we are taking on a role that rightfully belongs to God alone. James is very explicit on this point in v. 12. There is one Judge, he writes. That Judge is the one who is able to save and to destroy.

Third, James reminds us that we are in no position to judge. He writes in v. 12, "but who are you to judge your neighbor?" This is not a new idea. Jesus gave a similar command in Matthew 7:1-5, when He pointed out that we see specks in the eyes of others while ignoring the logs in our own eyes.

James is not arguing against church discipline. He is not arguing against helping a fellow believer, who has strayed, to return to faith. Indeed, he commends that type of behavior at the end of the letter (5:19-20). What he is warning against is sitting in judgement over our neighbors; criticizing them and making our own pronouncements about who is saved and who isn't. Thinking we know best is an aspect of the worldly wisdom James wrote about in chapter three.

The Arrogance of Planning (4:13-16)

James continues to warn against thinking we know best, with a focus on planning for the future. The phrase "come now," indicates a call to pay attention. James warns us not to depend on our own plans. He is not forbidding planning as a habit. Rather, he is attacking the mindset of ignoring God when we plan. The example James gives in v. 13 is that of a businessman in the ancient world, but it's not hard to picture the same scenario in the modern day. When we make our plans without relying on God, we reveal that we are using worldly wisdom and not heavenly wisdom. Proverbs 27:1 warns not to boast about tomorrow because we don't know the future. James reiterates that in v. 14 and adds a further comment on how transient our lives are. This verse echoes the analogy James gave in 1:10-11, that the businessman will fade away like a flower scorched by the sun.

So, what should we do instead? Stop boasting and bragging about our plans. Continue to plan, but shift our mindset. Recall that we are living in God's world and should seek His will. Stating this to ourselves helps to remind us. You may even find it helpful to state it aloud. After all, Jesus did not teach us to pray for all of our future plans at once. Instead, He taught us to pray for each day, day by day (Luke 11:3). This helps to remind us that no part of our lives is outside of God's control.

The Sin of Inaction (4:17)

The principle of v. 17 can apply to a wide variety of situations. The principle is also known as a sin of omission. The idea is not exclusively a biblical principle. Stoic philosopher and Roman emperor Marcus Aurelius makes the same point in his book Meditations (ix, 5). At the end of the passage on planning, James intends to apply the principle especially to the problem he just finished discussing.

The Folly of Riches (5:1-6)

James again calls us to pay attention by writing, "come now." James circles back in v. 2 to how he started the letter, saying earthly wealth will not last (1:9-11). Some scholars believe James is addressing non-believers in this passage. He doesn't refer to them as brothers, as he does throughout the letter. This passage has some of the strongest language in the entire book. It brings to mind the Old Testament prophets like Amos, Joel, and Hosea, declaring the judgment of God against the wealthy.

If James is addressing believers, this passage continues the theme of contrasting a reliance on earthly wisdom instead of heavenly wisdom. Such reliance is folly. The hoarding of earthly riches is fruitless, because all of it will rot and decay (Matt 6:19-21). A focus on wealth will also take our minds away from focusing on God and His will. A focus on wealth is self-centered by nature, and will cause us to place our needs above the needs of others. It may even cause us to cheat others or oppress them, as James notes in v. 4 and v. 6. It doesn't really matter if James was addressing believers or non-believers. We have this passage to remind us now to keep our focus where it belongs.

QUESTIONS FOR REFLECTION AND DISCUSSION

1. Have you ever been certain about something that turned out to be wrong?

2. Have you ever made a judgement about someone that damaged your relationship with that person?

3. Have you ever had your plans for the future overturned by circumstances outside your control?

4. How far into the future have you planned your life?

The Folly of Boasting

5. What four things are discussed in 4:13? What is bad about this type of planning?

6. Is all planning sinful? How can you balance planning and trusting God?

7. Can you think of a time when 4:17 was true of you?

8. Do you think 5:1-6 is directed at believers or non-believers? Explain.

9. Discuss how you can apply the wisdom from 5:1-6 this week.

10. In light of this chapter, do you think Christians should play the lottery? Explain why or why not.

Chapter Eight

Patience

(James 5:7-12)

In the last section, James discussed how the rich oppress the poor. He made this point early in the letter (2:6-7), and went into much greater detail in vv. 1-6 of this chapter. Now, James presents a solution. But it's not a solution many of us would embrace willingly. His solution is for us to be patient until the Lord's coming. Having just described the cruelty and oppression of the rich, James commands us to refrain from getting even ourselves and to wait for the return of the Messiah.

Patience does not come easy. It is, by definition, suffering or enduring something you don't want to endure. It's no surprise that the word "patient," meaning someone undergoing medical treatment, and "patience" come from the same Latin root. You don't develop patience when everything is going your way. You develop patience when unpleasant things are happening to you, and fixing them is beyond your control. James is circling back to the way he started the letter, noting that patience creates perseverance, and perseverance makes us mature and complete. If we have genuine faith, we will wait for Christ's second coming with steadfast hearts despite trials. To help inspire us to be patient, James gives us three models to emulate.

Practice Patience Like a Farmer (5:7-9)

Israel had two rainy seasons, one in the fall and one in the spring. Farmers would sow seeds just before the fall rainy season. The spring rains happened as the grain was maturing. Farmers had to wait for both rainy seasons to happen before harvesting their crops.

James assures us that the Lord is coming, and He will set things right. While we are waiting, we need to be patient both with non-believers who oppress us and fellow believers who irritate us (5:9).

Practice Patience Like the Prophets (5:10-11a)

God's prophets spoke His truth to the nation of Israel throughout the Old Testament. Their warnings and exhortations were often met with mistreatment and derision. Jeremiah was thrown into prison (Jer 32:2) and lowered into a dungeon (Jer 38:6) for speaking God's truth. Amos was threatened by the chief priest when he spoke against King

Jeroboam (Amos 7:10-13). Daniel was thrown into the lion's den for his steadfast worship of God (Dan 6). These men and many other prophets serve as models for us of patience while suffering for our belief in God. James reminds us that blessings come from such perseverance.

Practice Patience Like Job (5:11b)

James intentionally escalates his examples to a climax with Job. Farmers exercise patience against the elements. The prophets were patient in the face of antagonism and oppression. And then there's Job, being tormented by Satan himself. Each example builds in terms of the struggle to practice patience, but the result of perseverance also increases.

I wouldn't wish the trials of Job on anyone. He lost all of his wealth. His ten children died. He was stricken with illness. Despite all these trials, Job did not blame God for his suffering (Job 1:22). James reminds us that Job persevered and was blessed. God gave Job another ten children. He gave Job twice as much wealth as he had before (Job 42:10-17). Job's example teaches us that sometimes God allows us to endure suffering to test our faith. Job's story reminds us that knowing God is more important than having all the answers.

Don't Swear (5:12)

James returns to the theme of our speech from chapter three. It is especially tempting during times of suffering to curse and swear profanely, but that is not what James is referring to here. He is referring to the habit of casually giving oaths in daily life testifying to the truth of something. Jesus forbids swearing altogether (Matt 5:34-37). James echoes this prohibition with simple advice. Be so truthful, he says, that people believe you when you say "yes" or "no" without the need for an oath. Otherwise, you may find yourself sinning by taking the Lord's name in vain.

QUESTIONS FOR REFLECTION AND DISCUSSION

1. According to James, what should we patiently wait for?

2. How are we supposed to act while we're waiting?

3. Why are the prophets good examples of patience in the face of suffering?

4. Why do you think James uses Job as his example of perseverance?

5. Discuss an area of your life where you need God's help to persevere patiently.

6. James 5:9 mentions God as a Judge, while 5:11 mentions His mercy. Which have you been feeling more of in the last week? Explain.

7. Explain 5:12 in your own words. Why do you think James says we should follow this rule, "above all"?

Chapter Nine

Prayer

(James 5:13-18)

It is possible to write a book entirely devoted to the subject of prayer. Indeed, many theologians have done so. It is not my intent to attempt a project of that scope in this chapter. Instead, I want to point out three points which James makes about prayer. First, James urges us to pray in all circumstances. Next, he provides an example of the effectiveness of sincere prayer. Last, he provides thoughts on when prayer is not effective.

Pray in All Circumstances (5:13-16a)

We should pray when we are suffering or in trouble. The verb here is the same as the word used in v. 10 to refer to the suffering experienced by the prophets. When we face adversity, we should not grumble (v. 9). Instead, we should pray. Prayer is not just for times of adversity, however. We should sing praises to God when we are happy as well (Col 3:16). I think this is even harder sometimes. It's easy to call on God when times are tough. It's harder to remember to praise Him when things are going well.

James addresses not only individual prayer, but communal prayer as well. Throughout the book, James notes the need to worship together as one body unified in Christ. If one member of the body is sick or suffering, the whole body should rally to that person. The anointing with oil is more medical than spiritual. The main "active ingredient" is prayer.

It bears mentioning, however, than not all prayers result in healing bodily illness. Some people remain sick. Some people do not get better. James says, "the prayer of faith will save the one who is sick, and the Lord will raise him up" (5:15). The word "save" here is associated with both physical healing and spiritual salvation. It's the same word used in James 2:14, when James writes, "can that word save him?" Similarly, the word "raise" also has a double meaning. It can mean to get out of bed, or it can refer to the resurrection. James is once again pointing out that heavenly matters such as salvation are more important than earthly matters such as physical well-being.

Can our prayers move someone to repent? Can our prayers help someone to be forgiven and to experience God's grace? Can our prayers help to heal someone? The answer to all is an emphatic "yes!" As proof of that, James offers an Old Testament example to illustrate the effectiveness of prayer.

The Effect of Sincere Prayer (5:16b-18)

The word "prayer" is used five times in vv. 13-16. The first four times it's used, the same word is used. Now, at the end of v. 16, James switches to a different word. He writes, "the prayer of a righteous man is powerful and effective" (5:16b). The word used for "prayer" here has the connotation of pleading or begging to have an urgent need met. And James says this type of prayer "has great power." Take Elijah, for example.

The story of Elijah is found in First Kings, chapters 17 and 18. Elijah prayed and it did not rain for three and a half years. First Kings 17:1 doesn't explicitly say Elijah prayed, but it is clear from the context. Then, in First Kings 18:36-37, Elijah prays and God sent rain on the land after sending fire from the sky to light the sacrificial altar. Jewish tradition at the time revered Elijah. Two apocryphal books, the Second Book of Esdras and the Book of Sirach, both tell this story with an emphasis on the power of Elijah.

James puts the emphasis on God. There was nothing magical about Elijah. He was a prophet, but he was also a man. He sinned and had flaws. His power came from his reliance on God, not on anything that was part of his own nature. James encourages us with this reminder. Our prayers don't work because of us. They work because we are aligning ourselves to God's will.

Ineffective Prayer

What about when our prayers don't work? James has already addressed this at different points throughout the letter. We cannot expect an answer when we doubt God (1:6-7). We should not expect an answer when we refuse to repent and approach God in humility (1:21). We will not receive an answer when we don't even ask, or when we ask with the wrong motives (4:2-3). God is not a genie in a bottle who does our bidding.

QUESTIONS FOR REFLECTION AND DISCUSSION

1. What causes you to resist praying?

2. What prayers are you "double-minded" about?

3. Can you recall an instance when the timing of your prayer did not align with God's timing?

4. Do you think of others as being better at praying than you?

5. How does the example of Elijah in vv. 17-18 encourage you?

6. Discuss some specific changes you can make to your prayer life in the coming week.

Chapter Ten
Saving the Wanderers
(James 5:19-20)

As James noted in 3:2, "we all stumble in many ways." Now, in the final two verses of his letter, James talks about what to do when someone "wanders from the truth" (5:19). It should be pretty obvious – you go get them and bring them back!

Save a Wandering Brother (5:19-20)

Since James uses the phrase "my brothers," it's clear he's addressing believers. There is a question, however, about whether the wanderer is a believer or not. James says the person who brings back a wanderer will "save his soul from death" (5:20). This implies the soul won't be saved if the wanderer doesn't return. Thus the question of whether the wanderer is a believer or not is based on the concept of whether a person can lose salvation or not.

The theological term for this concept is apostasy. This term comes from a Greek word meaning "to stand away from." Some denominations maintain that Christians can stray so far from the path of righteousness that they lose their salvation. One passage that seems to support this idea is First Timothy 1:18-20. In that passage, Paul writes, "This charge I entrust to you, Timothy, my child, in accordance with the prophecies previously made about you, that by them you may wage the good warfare, holding faith and a good conscience. By rejecting this, some have made shipwreck of their faith, among whom are Hymenaeus and Alexander, whom I have handed over to Satan that they may learn not to blaspheme." By saying Hymenaeus and Alexander, among others, had shipwrecked their faith, Paul is admitting that they had faith to begin with but lost it.

Other denominations maintain such a person was never a believer to begin with. To support this, one could look at First John 2:19. John says those who departed were not believers to begin with. In Romans 8:38-39, Paul writes that nothing can separate us from God's love, not even ourselves. Therefore, someone who has salvation cannot lose it. But it is possible to appear to be saved and not, in fact, be saved. James talks about this at the beginning of the book when he talks about those who have "stood the test" (1:12).

Personally, I believe it is not possible to lose salvation. I also believe, however, that it is possible for a believer to stray far from the path of righteousness. After all, James addressed his letter to fellow believers. He then proceeded to talk to us about partiality, anger management, harmful speech, and apathy when faced with those in need. Not exactly role models of Christian behavior, right?

Whether you believe someone can lose salvation or not, the solution in both cases is the same. When someone wanders, James urges us to "bring him back" (5:19). How do we do that?

Bringing him back implies that we don't wait for the person to come to us. We seek him out. We shouldn't shy away from helping the poor and the hungry (2:15-16). Similarly, we shouldn't shy away from speaking the truth to help others come back to God. We can condemn the bad behavior, but we shouldn't condemn the person (4:11-12). We provide an example of wisdom and understanding (3:13). We draw near to God and encourage others to do the same (4:8). In this way, we demonstrate genuine faith through our works. The result will bring glory to God!

QUESTIONS FOR REFLECTION AND DISCUSSION

1. Have you ever wandered away from the faith? Who or what brought you back?

2. How does bringing someone back demonstrate the body of Christ?

3. What will you do differently as a result of studying James?

Conclusion

The book of James ends abruptly. It doesn't have the long, draw-out good-bye feel of a Pauline epistle. It doesn't have the "grace be with you all" of Hebrews 13:25. It doesn't even have the perfunctory "Amen" of Second Peter or Jude. The only other New Testament letter that ends this abruptly is First John.

As much as I love the book of James, I don't want to end this book in the same way. I hope this book has helped you to delve deeper into the rich theology of James. I pray you don't see it as an "epistle of straw," but as a concise treatise on developing genuine faith.

May God's grace be with you all. Amen.

NOTES

NOTES

NOTES

About the Author

Ed Cox is a veteran and the author of four books which have sold thousands of copies. He served in the U.S. Army for 26 years, rising to the rank of Colonel. From 2008 to 2011, he was an assistant professor of American Politics at the United States Military Academy, West Point, NY.

Ed has a bachelor's degree from the United States Military Academy and two master's degrees from Syracuse University's Maxwell School. He is currently pursuing a Master's of Divinity from Southern Baptist Theological Seminary.

About the Font

P22 Franklin Caslon was designed by Paul D. Hunt and Richard Kegler at the P22 Type Foundry. This font uses digitized impressions of printing done by Benjamin Franklin's printing office, circa 1750. Franklin used a typeset based on the work of British typefounder William Caslon.

www.ingramcontent.com/pod-product-compliance
Lightning Source LLC
Chambersburg PA
CBHW020429010526
44118CB00010B/493